CW00567325

Magical Moments
Childhood Memories
of eastmoor

Taken from the diary of Jenny Jarvis
With illustrations by her brother Jimmy

David T Craggs

ISBN No. 1-905546-08-4
978-1-905546-08-4

Published by Write Books CPR Ltd
Ferrybridge, West Yorkshire
www.writebooks.org.uk

About the Author

David Craggs was born on the Eastmoor Estate in 1937. He was educated at Eastmoor Junior School and Queen Elizabeth Grammar School.

After qualifying as a teacher in 1961 he commenced his career at Ings road Secondary school, Wakefield. In 1968 he was appointed Head of Science at the newly opened Eastmoor High School and completed twenty-one years there before taking early retirement in 1989.

He and his wife Jean now live in the Yorkshire coastal village of Tunstall, where most of his time is occupied by being a Parish Councillor and Governor of two local schools.

But first a word from the author

Before reading the diary entries I feel that it would help if you had some idea of what it was like to live as a thirteen year old child on the Eastmoor Estate in 1947.

Please read on, and compare it with your lifestyle today.

Eastmoor is an area on the eastern side of the City of Wakefield in West Yorkshire. It appears on old maps and at some time in the past there may well have been a moor there, but certainly not today.

The large housing estate where Jenny and Jimmy lived was built in the early 1930s. Many of the families that moved there had lived in old Victorian back-to-back houses, with little natural light, outside toilets and no gardens. Although the houses were very modern at that time most of today's children would have found them a little strange.

The living room had a large coal fire with an equally large oven at the side of it that could be heated by directing the flames from the fire round it. The wood floor was covered in linoleum, or lino, as it was referred to then. It was not unlike the vinyl floors that we see today in some kitchens. There was always a rug in front of the fireplace but rarely anywhere else.

The furniture usually consisted of a three piece suite and a dining room suite, the latter having a sideboard, a huge piece of furniture with a set of drawers in its centre and cupboards either side.

The kitchen was very basic. In the corner, next to the window, was a large, deep, square sink, with a draining board coming down to it. Hot and cold water were supplied by two exposed pipes coming down from the ceiling. Tucked under the draining board was a large electric boiler for washing clothes in, and at the other end of it was positioned a very basic electric cooker with a kettle usually standing on the top.

There was, of course, no refrigerator. Food was kept cool by placing it on a cold slab in the pantry, a small recess, attached to the kitchen. In summer the milk bottles had to be covered with a damp cloth to keep them cool. Preserving food was not a big problem, however, because fresh milk was delivered daily, and mothers shopped on an almost daily basis for meat and fish, fruit and vegetables, and bread, often walking over a mile to do so. They had to buy their food using the coupons in their ration books, for at that time food rationing was in operation, as was the rationing of sweets, furniture and clothes.

Leading off the kitchen was the bathroom, with its large iron bath and porcelain washbasin. In order to go to the toilet you had to go out of the back door and across an open porch, not very pleasant when rain was being driven onto the back of the house by a cold northerly wind. It had to be a quick dash, there and back, for when nature called, one had to go. A second door was sometimes placed across the opening.

Both front and back doors had large locks, and hence large keys. Keys were therefore rarely carried around. Children never did so. If parents were out when their children arrived home from school the back door key was usually hidden somewhere. Jenny and Jimmy always knew that their key would be behind the toilet cistern. Other children also knew the hiding place, but there were never any break ins.

There were three bedrooms upstairs. The front one was the largest and always the parents' room. The two rear bedrooms were usually fought over by the children. The larger one often had a double bed in it, and it was by far the warmer because it contained the airing cupboard. In there the water, heated by the boiler behind the downstairs fire, was stored in a large tank called the cylinder. Above the cylinder were open shelves where clothes and bedding could be aired off - not unlike they are today in many modern homes.

There were, of course, no electric blankets. On cold winter nights a heavy overcoat was often thrown across the bed. Hot water bottles were also used, but were renowned for leaking. Sometimes one of the hot iron shelves was taken from the oven, wrapped in a sheet or towel, and placed in the bed, just where the feet would go. Unfortunately the shelves soon cooled down. The bedroom floors were also covered with linoleum, with the odd rug placed here and there.

Every house had, and still has, a small front garden and a long back garden. The man of the house took a great pride in his gardens, regularly mowing lawns and clipping privet hedges. Every block of two houses had an air raid shelter in the back garden. This was made of steel and was called an 'Anderson', presumably after the man who invented it. It was constructed in a hole in the ground, then covered with soil and grassed over. One or two bombs were dropped on Wakefield during the Second World War, but none fell on Eastmoor. Nevertheless, when the siren went everybody went down into the shelter, complete with gas mask, and the door was closed. Candles or oil lamps provided the light. Everybody then waited for the 'all clear' siren to go. At the end of the war the shelters were eventually dismantled and either taken away or rebuilt as garden sheds and garages. Most back gardens were divided halfway down, usually by a trellis with roses climbing up it, or a small privet hedge. The lower half was often used to cultivate vegetables, a practice that had been encouraged during the war years to make the nation self sufficient in foods such as potatoes, peas, onions and cabbage.

Since every house had a coal fire, coal had to be delivered or collected from the Pit Yard. Since the Jarvis family lived just opposite the yard, once a fortnight Mr Jarvis went across with his sack cart and bought two sacks of coal. On the occasions that his dad was at work, or had a bad back, it was Jimmy's job to fetch the coal. In his case it had to be one sack at a time. The coal was stored in an outside coalhouse, and sometimes had to be fetched in during atrocious weather. Mrs Jarvis often told her son to fetch a bucket of coal in at the same as going to the toilet. No point in getting wet twice.

All children on Eastmoor up to the age of eleven attended one of four schools, none of which was actually on the estate itself. They were Eastmoor Junior, St Andrew's, St Mary's and St Austin's. Jimmy, Jenny and most of their friends attended Eastmoor Junior, which was about a mile away from where they lived. They always went and returned on their own. Parents accompanying children to school was unheard of except during the first few days after admission at three or four years of age. Many children went home for dinner, so on a schoolday they were walking in the region of four miles. When the children changed school at eleven their new school was even further away. In fact Jimmy's new school was in the centre of Wakefield. Luckily for him, it wasn't long before he got his first bike.

So what did Jenny, Jimmy and their friends do for entertainment? The answer was very little, at least in the home. This was the main reason why they spent so much of their time playing out. There was little to stay in for. Any homework was done before tea or before breakfast the following morning, then it was out to play, regardless of the time of year. When dark, Mrs Jarvis's instructions were simple. 'Don't go out of the street, and don't get into mischief.' This second instruction was obviously aimed at her son. During the summer months the equally simple instruction was, 'Be in by nine o'clock. Not a minute later.' In that time one could easily get down to Little Wood, build a den and still get back in time. No children possessed a watch so they had to just guess at the time. During weekends and school holidays one played out from morning till night, only returning to 'base' when one was hungry, tired or if injured in some way. But in spite of all the freedom the children had and the silly things they sometimes did, accidents rarely happened. Was it just luck, or did they really know how to look after themselves? It was probably a combination of the two, and who knows? Maybe a guardian angel was always there, looking over them. Could the fact that so many of these children reached adulthood relatively unscathed be evidence that there may just be a God after all? It at least bears thinking about.

But what happened when it rained? The weather wasn't perfect all the time but, looking back through rose coloured glasses, it did seem pretty good most of the time. Well, children read, wrote and drew, and most children were pretty good at all three. Jenny was an exceptional creative writer, whereas Jimmy was an excellent drawer. Both were avid readers.

They played games such as ludo, snakes and ladders, and cards. Since mum was always baking, Jenny became a dab hand at mixing dough for bread, and icing buns and cakes. On the other hand Jimmy would help his dad with a bit of DIY. That's when he wasn't in the shed, dismantling his bike for the umpteenth time, and reassembling it, usually with one or two bits to spare. There was, of course, no television, the first ones appearing in homes in the early 1950s. So, children listened to the wireless - a large wooden box, usually standing in the corner. If one could see inside, one would see the glass valves, glowing like electric light bulbs. The front had knobs, as radios do today, and a large tuning dial with the names of every major city in the world on it. The highlight of the day was listening to 'Dick Barton - Special Agent' at quarter to seven in the evening. He was the equivalent of today's James Bond. All outside play was suspended. It didn't matter who was on at tigs, or who had just scored a try at rugby, play had to stop for fifteen minutes to listen to Dick Barton.

There were comedy programmes to listen to, and music too. Rock-and-Roll hadn't quite arrived, but the music of the day was already heading that way, the presence of American soldiers in this country during the war having changed, forever, the sort of music we listened to. Later in the evening a ghost story may be on the wireless. Dad would turn out the lights and the family would listen by only the glow of the fire. Going to bed after it was always a spooky experience, and beds were looked under.

Almost every dad had a fulltime job, often working long hours or shifts. Mr Jarvis, working as a nurse at the Mental Hospital, as it was called then, the name being later changed to Stanley Royd, worked eight hour shifts, but many men worked even longer hours. Most mums stayed at home and looked after the family. But even then they seemed to have little time to themselves. As soon as they had washed up the breakfast pots they were off to the shops for something for dinner, which had to be cooked by the time their children came home from school at about twenty past twelve. After washing up the dinner pots some baking had to be done for tea. Washday was always on a Monday, and since they didn't have time to shop or prepare something for dinner, the left overs from Sunday dinner were used up, so cold beef was usually on the menu, along with 'bubble- and- squeak', a mixture of mashed potato and cabbage, fried in a pan. It was a good way to get children to eat that most hated of vegetables, cabbage.

What is known as credit today was known as hire purchase then, but most families saved for what they wanted, consequently clothes and furniture were only replaced when the need to do so was there. And on some occasions the change made a big difference to family life, for example, when the black iron fire range was replaced by a bright, spanking new tiled fireplace, and the old, worn linoleum was replaced by wall-to-wall carpet. Those families who made such changes were usually referred to as being 'posh'.

Many families went on holiday for one week a year, usually to the East Coast of Yorkshire - Bridlington, Filey and Scarborough being favourite places. Jenny and Jimmy Jarvis loved Brid. as it was affectionately known. They spent their annual holiday there seven years running, and never got tired of it. In fact on more than one occasion Jimmy shed a tear or two because he didn't want to go home. The family used to pack their suitcases, then walk down to Kirkgate Station to catch the through train to Brid. The time eventually came when a bus service started to run to the East Coast from Wakefield, and it was much cheaper than by train. So the family travelled by bus, all except Jimmy. He was terribly travel sick on the bus, but not on the train, so he travelled alone, being picked up at Bridlington railway station by his parents and sister. The family always stayed at the same guesthouse, but the meal arrangements were very strange. One 'kept oneself'. This meant that Mrs Jarvis bought all the food in, shopping every morning, and the landlady would then cook it. She would even fry the fish that Mr Jarvis had caught earlier in the day in Bridlington Bay. Jimmy had a 'love-hate' relationship with fishing. On the one hand he loved to go out on a fishing coble with his dad, 'Hilary' being his favourite. Dad knew the skipper and they always got the best spot in the boat, but he was usually seasick, unless the sea was as flat as a millpond. While the 'men' were fishing, Jenny and her mother would either sit on the beach in deckchairs, reading, knitting, writing cards or simply taking in the view, or they would head for the shops.

I have tried to paint you a picture of what life was like for Jenny and Jimmy Jarvis back in 1947. It is now time for you to read the thirty two entries that I have chosen from Jenny's diary, and to study the excellent drawings that her brother, Jimmy, did for her to accompany her entries. All but one of thirty two describe outdoor activities, they being far more interesting than those carried out indoors, usually because of bad weather, or being kept in for some terrible crime, such as cheeking one of the neighbours. Please read on and enjoy, and don't forget to refer to Jimmy's map in order to see where the various activities took place.

(All the names of people have been changed to protect the innocent, and not so innocent)

What one or more of us did -

Sledged down Park Lodge Lane. 1

Built a snow den in the Tip bank 2

Sledged down the Old Quarry 3

Fell down Windhill Brick Works Quarry. 4

Hitched a ride on a lorry carrying sand 5

Walked the long wall 6

Long jumped down the Old Quarry 7

Telephoned across Gelder's Field 8

Fed the horses down at Kirkgate Station 9

Hunted for clay pipes on the canal bank 10

Attended the Junior Club at the Empire. 11

Hitched a ride on a coal train 12

Played tigs on the King George slide 13

Swam in the hot water pond at Parkhills pit 14

Trainspotted down at Kirkgate station 15

Built a treehouse down at Little Wood 16

Built a great den in the hedge along Gelder's Field 17

Played Peggy and Sticks in the street 18

Swam in the sand quarry. 19

Escaped from Devil's Hollow 20

Played a prank on the driver of the coal train..................21

Trainspotted at the Ninety Nine Arches 22

Collected conkers in the Mental Hospital grounds 23

Explored the 'tombs' at the County Hospital.. 24

Slid down the pit slag heap on a sheet of tin 25

Saw a film on Robin Hood, and pretended to be him.. 26

Potato picked down near Parkhills Pit... 27

Hitched a ride on a barge to the aqueduct.........................28

Built and lit our fire on Bonfire Night 29

Listened to the BBC on our crystal set 30

Turned off all the gas lamps on Park Lodge Lane 31

Opened our presents on Christmas Day 32

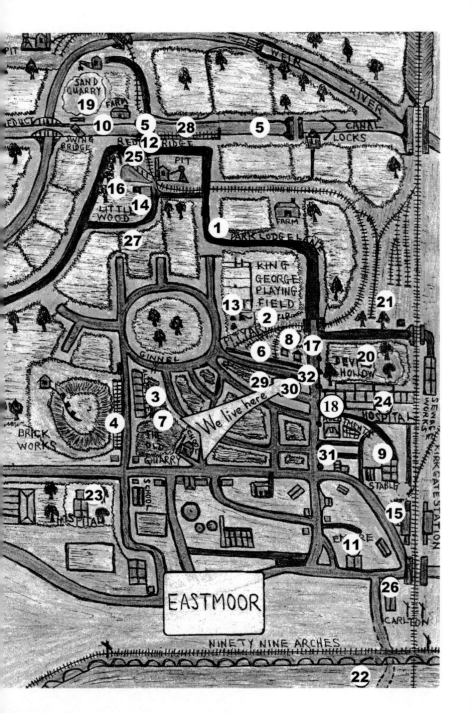

12th January

Sunday

Dear Diary Look at 1 on our map

There has been a keen frost during the night and when we walked on the snow this morning it crunched. Dave Crosby has told us that the whole of Park Lodge Lane, right down to the canal, is covered with ice because the water that drips from the sand quarry lorries has frozen. Our Jimmy got out our sledges from the shed and we set off. We decided to cut across King George playing field and found it difficult to walk, our wellies sinking into the deep snow. When we reached the top of Park Lodge Lane we could see that a train of sledges, formed by the older lads, was halfway down the hill. Some of our Jimmy's mates were already forming the next train. He pushed my sledge into the middle and told me to lie flat on it. He joined the train behind me. We then linked up. I grabbed the ankles of the lad in front of me. Our Jimmy grabbed my ankles. The others in the train did the same.

When we were ready the last lad somehow pushed off, grabbing the ankles of the lad in front as he did so. The train started to move slowly onto the slope, then picked up speed. The lad at the front had one of those sledges that you can steer and the rest of us somehow followed him. The last lad was supposed to slow us down, but in no time at all we seemed to be doing a hundred miles an hour. We sped across the railway track and headed for the canal fence. How could we possibly stop? I didn't think we could. Then the first lad steered his sledge into the thick snow at the side of the lane and rolled off. The rest of us did the same, some shooting across to the other side of the lane. We all seemed okay so we grabbed the rope on our sledges and headed back up the hill. I soon got tired and stopped to rest, but the lads would not wait for me. They wanted to form another train, with Jimmy at the front. I decided not to join in. I had no intention of killing myself by shooting through the canal fence and drowning in the freezing water. They

13

set off and I decided to sledge down on my own. Soon I found myself catching them up. I had to steer into the thick snow at the side in order to stop. I looked up just in time to see Jimmy's head disappearing through the fence, Fortunately the lad behind stopped him from going down the canal bank.

Mam said "We all know that our Jimmy's not right in the head, but does my only daughter have to behave in the same crazy way? Heaven forbid".

My mam can't accept that her only daughter is a bit of a tomboy and wants to prove that she can do all the things that her crazy brother and his mates can do. Dad's different. He understands. In fact he secretly encourages me.

19th January
Sunday
Dear Diary   *Look at 2 on our map*
It has snowed heavily through the night, and when I looked out of my bedroom window this morning I saw that Mr Craven's car next door had almost disappeared. Our Jimmy got up early and

had already made a snowman in the garden by the time I had got up. He'd got some pieces of coal from the coalhouse for the eyes, nose and mouth, and had even pinched my dad's cap and scarf from the coat pegs behind the front door. After breakfast we got our sledges out of the shed and pulled them into the street. Our Jimmy called for Dave and Tom Crosby, and I called for Betty Smith who lives next door to us. We then set off for Park Lodge Lane where we had sledged a few days ago. As we started across King George playing field we saw some kids playing on the bank leading down to the Tip. The snow had drifted over the bank during the night and was now about six feet deep. We pushed our sledges to one side and soon found that we could burrow into the snowdrift and make a den without the snow caving in. It was like an igloo but not made of blocks of snow like the ones you see in the books at school. You know, like the ones that eskimos live in. Anyway, we had just made our snow den big enough for our Jimmy and Tom to get inside when we saw Alan Knott and Richard James coming across the field They saw our snow den and jumped on the top of it making it cave in, they then went away laughing. As soon as they'd gone we started to dig another and bigger den further along the bank where the snow was even deeper. When we had finished it, it was so big that all five of us could get inside. We thought it would be cold but it wasn't. It started to snow again and soon a blizzard was blowing across the playing field but we were warm and protected in our snow den. We returned to the bank after dinner but someone had smashed our snow den in. I bet it was Jamesy and Knotty. They always like to spoil things. Only last week they smashed up Denis Kelly's bike because he wouldn't let them have a ride on it.

Mam said "Next time Richard James picks on you, our Jimmy, or smashes up anything that belongs to you I want you to punch him in the face. I'll get your dad to give you some boxing lessons".

I can't wait for round one. Dad's a real hard case and used to play for Wakefield Trinity. Mind you, if he can teach our Jimmy how to box, maybe Jimmy will be able to punch Richard James in the face. It may then stop him picking on us. He's a bully and most of the kids hate him. Our Jimmy would be a hero.

22nd February
Saturday
Dear Diary   *Look at 3 on our map*
It has again snowed heavily through the night and when our Jimmy
went out onto the street with his sledge he saw his mate Ronnie
Jaques, who had just delivered our newspaper. Dave said that
everyone would be sledging this morning at the old quarry. Our
Jimmy tried to sneak off without me but my mam called him back
to clean his teeth. As we made our way up Parkgate Avenue Dave
and Tom Crosby joined us with their sledges. It was difficult walking
up Watson Crescent but we made it to the top and walked through
the ginnel and onto the old quarry. There seemed to be every kid
on the estate there, most with a sledge. One or two kids have posh
sledges that have been bought at Hayley's sports shop in town.
They are made of wood and have shiny metal runners. It's even
possible to steer them. Other sledges have been made by the kids'
dads who work at the foundry on Peterson Road. They are the

17

lightest and the fastest. Mick Everson has one of these. Mine and Jimmy's sledges were made by our dad, who works at the hospital as a nurse. They are made of wood and the runners are made from bucket handles. I don't think mam knows yet since she hasn't had to wash the steps lately. All the big lads, like Alan Knott and Richard James, set off first. They wanted a clear run, but both fell off halfway down. We all cheered. Then it was our Jimmy's turn. He reached the bottom then rolled off to stop him hitting the wall of St Andrew's School. As all the lads were walking slowly back up the slope me and a couple of mates decided to have a go. I went first, but panicked as my sledge picked up speed. I tried to slow it down by digging my heels into the snow. I slowed down a bit but then veered off to the left and slid into Richard James, knocking him over. He was about to hit me when he realized I was a girl. He walked away limping. We spent all morning sledging, and returned home soaked to the skin. Mam wasn't best pleased when our Jimmy placed the clothes horse in front of the fire with our wet clothes on it.

Mam said "You've got to remember that your dad's a nurse not a welder Think yourselves lucky that he's built you a sledge at all. And by the way, our Jimmy. I don't suppose you know why my two best buckets have no handles".

Our Jimmy was about to tell her when I kicked him under the table. There was no point in getting dad into trouble. When all said and done he had made two sledges for us, and he had to use whatever he could get his hands on. I told mam that the handles had probably fallen off, and were somewhere on the shed floor.

8th April
Tuesday
Dear Diary   *Look at 4 on our map*
Our Jimmy nearly got killed today. We were walking along Queen Elizabeth Road on our way home from Auntie May's, where we'd

had our tea, when he decided to squeeze through a gap in the fence surrounding the quarry at Windhill Brickworks. Jimmy had noticed that the trucks at the bottom had been loaded up with clay and were being pulled up to the top, and he wanted to get a better look. Suddenly the edge where he was standing gave way and he disappeared from view. I was convinced that he had fallen to the bottom and was dead. At first I didn't dare to look over the edge, but plucked up enough courage to do so. I knew that I was also in danger of falling if I got too near so I laid down, edged forward and peered over. Our Jimmy had been lucky. Very lucky indeed. He had only fallen about ten feet and onto a grassy ledge no more than two feet wide. As he laid there he said he was all right and told me to get help. I didn't half breathe a sigh of relief. Mam would have killed me if he'd been dead. At first I didn't know what to do, but then I saw an old man working in the allotments on the other side of the road. I crossed, told him what had happened and asked him if he could help. He said that he probably could, disappeared into his shed and came out with a coil of rope. We crossed the road, but being old and quite fat he could not get through

or over the fence. He therefore had to pass the rope through the gap to me and I lowered it down to our Jimmy. The man shouted to him to tie it tightly round his waist, which he did. Jimmy's good at knots. He used to be a boy scout. The man then pulled on the rope. It took a great effort because he was quite an old man. Slowly Jimmy scrambled up the slippery clay face to the top and climbed over the edge. Although his clothes were covered in clay he seemed all right. As the man coiled up his rope he gave our Jimmy a right telling off, stressing how daft he was. I nodded in agreement. We thanked the man and Jimmy said that he would never ever do anything so daft again, but I told the man that he would.

Mam said "You shouldn't have spoken to the man on the allotment, our Jenny. There are some very funny men around, and they like talking to young girls. You should have gone to the phone box close by and called the fire brigade".

I pointed out that the man was old and looked friendly. She said that they always do. She didn't say what the funny men talked about, but Janine Burton said that it was probably something to do with S-E-X, you know, that word that is never spoken in our house.

18th April
Friday
Dear Diary   *Look at 5 on our map*
Today our Jimmy said that he was going down to the canal with
Dave Crosby to see the barges. The lock keeper had told them
yesterday that a big petrol tanker would be coming up to the storage
depot near Brothertons Chemical works today. It would be passing
through his lock at ten thirty. When Jimmy called on Dave, Dave's
mam wouldn't let him out because he was in late last night. Jimmy
was real disappointed so I decided to go with him. Normally he
wouldn't have let me but today he did because there was no one
else. As we crossed King George playing field we bumped into
Alan Knott and Richard James. I didn't want to tell them where
we were going, but my big mouth brother did. Maybe he was
scared of them, but I wasn't, I wasn't best pleased when they said
they were coming with us. We walked down Park Lodge Lane
and onto the towpath of the canal. Alan Knott had a watch and at
exactly half past ten we saw the tanker in the distance crossing the
Stanley Ferry aqueduct. It was huge, I guessed about the same

length as Sun Lane Baths, which I know is a hundred feet long. Know-all Richard James said it was only fifty, but he was miles out. As the tanker passed us a huge wave washed onto the towpath, soaking our shoes. The captain, if that's who he was, smiled and waved. Jimmy shouted "Give us a lift mister", but the tanker pushed on towards the lock gates, which were already open. It disappeared under the railway bridge. At that point Alan Knott and Richard James decided to leave us and head for Little Wood where, according to them, they were building a den. Our Jimmy wanted to go with them, but I didn't so he had to stay with me. If he'd left me down there alone, mam would have killed him. She'd already said that we must stick together. Anyway, it started to rain quite heavily and I suggested that we sheltered under the Red Bridge. Then we saw a lorry approaching with a load of sand. The driver wound down his window and asked where we lived. I said near the County Hospital. He pushed open the door and we both scrambled in, He dropped us off at the end of our street. Our mam was surprised that we weren't soaked to the skin. Jimmy explained.

Mam said "When you're out on your own you must never accept lifts from strangers, especially you, our Jenny. Funny things can happen to girls".

Mam has this annoying habit of telling us things that we shouldn't do and places were we shouldn't go, especially me, but never explains why. She says she will tell me when I'm older, but I bet I'm twenty five before she does.

24th April

Thursday

Dear Diary   *Look at 6 on our map*

This evening me, our Jimmy and his mates Dave and Tom Crosby walked the full length of the long wall. At the end of all the back gardens on one side of our street there is a long high wall. It separates the gardens from the Pit Yard, although it isn't a pit yard really because there isn't a pit, but coal from Parkhills Pit comes there by rail and is loaded into lorries and taken away. Anyway, you can get onto the wall by climbing up the yard gate and striding across. There is nowhere else you can get onto it without a ladder. At a guess the wall is three hundred yards long, ten feet high and only about nine inches wide. We had seen the older lads walk the

length of the wall on many occasions, but we had never dared to try it ourselves until today. We climbed up the pit yard gate and moved onto the wall. I was surprised how high it seemed when I looked down. It's funny how looking down always seems different to looking up. I was also surprised how narrow it was. Nine inches seems a lot until you're standing on a wall nine inches wide.

All four of us started to walk slowly along the wall. Dave was in the lead. I was third. We had only gone a few yards when I nearly fell off. I sat down feeling very frightened. The rest stopped and

our Jimmy came and sat at my side, trying to calm me down. Jim spotted a ladder propped up against the wall in Mr Hudson's garden. If I could edge my way a few yards along the wall I would be able to climb down. I reached the ladder and tried to get to my feet.

Our Jimmy helped me. It was then that I decided to go on because I knew that if I managed to reach the end I would be the first girl in our street to do so. As we passed Alan Brown's house he came out and told us to get off his wall. He thought that his dad owned the bit at the bottom of his garden, but he didn't. He picked up a stone and threw it at Tom, nearly knocking him off. We then passed Mrs Gilbert's house. She came out to hang up some washing. She smiled and waved, and told us to be careful. Eventually we reached the end. Getting off was quite easy. We first sat on the wall then lowered ourselves down, and dropped the final few feet onto a grassy bank. We had done it.

Mam said "If Mrs Asquith had seen you she'd have gone to the phone box and called the police. You'd have all been locked up. And rightly so".

I don't think our mam likes us really because she's always saying that we should be locked up. Only last night she told our Jimmy that he should be because he rode home from Auntie May's in the dark without any lights.

7th May
Wednesday
Dear Diary   *Look at 7 on our map*
Our Jimmy is always talking about long jumping at the old quarry.

Mind you, he's always talking daft. My mam says that it's just the way he is. Anyway, this evening he showed me what he meant. He called for Dave and Tom Crosby and I called for Betty Smith. The five of us walked up our street, crossed onto Watson Crescent and went through the ginnel to the quarry. My dad said that it had been a brickworks like the one on the other side of Queen Elizabeth Road. It was now a dumping ground for all sorts of things.

Jim took us to where the long jumping takes place. It was a large steep sandy slope, but the sand was black, not like the sandy coloured sand you see at Bridlington or Blackpool. Dave said that he'd seen a lorry from Fox's Foundry tipping the black sand there. He says the sand is used to make casts. I don't understand what he means, and I bet he doesn't either. I've only heard of plaster casts, like the one I had when I broke my arm. Anyway, he showed me what to do. He walked back about ten yards from the edge, ran as fast as he could towards it and jumped as far as he could. Because of the slope he was able to jump a long way. Tom stuck a stick in the sand where his brother landed. Our Jimmy jumped next but didn't jump as far. Tom didn't either. I wanted to have a go, and yet I didn't, so Betty went next. She's the same age as Dave but is taller and has longer legs. When she took off she seemed to be in the air for ages. She landed about a foot past Dave's stick. It was now my turn. Betty had beaten the lads. Could I? I've always been able to run faster than our Jimmy so I walked back to the spot where Betty started her run, and set off. I quickly reached the edge and took off into space, staring at the town hall clock in the distance. I also seemed to be in the air for ages. Dave stuck a stick into the sand where I had landed, and guess what? I'd beaten both our Jimmy and Tom. They tried again but still couldn't reach my stick. As we made our way home me and Betty walked together, pleased with ourselves. Our Jimmy, Dave and Tom walked behind, sulking. Boys hated being beaten by girls, at anything.

Mam said "If you two ever come home again covered in black sand both of you will wash your own clothes for a month. You Jimmy can do yours on the washboard, and you, our Jenny can use the dolly tub, and you can do the ironing too".

I smiled at our Jimmy because I'd seen dad give our old washboard and dolly tub to the rag and bone man the other day, and only yesterday the iron blew up.

8th June
Monday
Dear Diary   *Look at 8 on our map*
Mick Peterson called at our house today with the crazy idea that
you can make a telephone by tying some string between two tins
and pulling the string tight. If you then speak into one tin a person
at the other end can hear if they hold the tin to their ear. We decided

to give it a try. Our Jimmy found a ball of string in the shed. Mick
had already searched their dustbin and found an empty soup tin. I
persuaded my mam to empty a tin of pears into a dish and let me
have the empty tin. Jimmy punched a hole in the bottom of each tin
with a hammer and a nail. I then threaded the string through the
holes and tied a large knot at the ends. It was now time to try it out.
The three of us went up to Gelder's field where the grass is about
three feet tall. Jimmy crouched down and held one of the tins to his
ear. I walked away from him until the string was tight. He must
have been at least twenty yards away. I too crouched down. Jimmy
then shouted his name into the tin. I got right excited when I heard

it. It was then my turn to shout my name into the tin. This time Mick placed his ear to the tin and listened. He then shouted across, telling me what I had said. We had proved that our telephone worked. When dad got home from work we told him about it. He just smiled, then disappeared. He came back with a large coil of wire and something he called a pair of earphones. He told us that he'd bought them at the Army and Navy stores in order to make our Jimmy a crystal set. He first separated the two earphones, then connected them to the ends of the wire. It was now time to try out our new telephone. Again we went to Gelder's field. Mick walked away with one earphone. Me and our Jimmy listened with the other. This time Mick was at least fifty yards away. He spoke into his earphone and Jimmy heard his name clearly. I also heard mine. Mick then said that he was going to listen to Dick Barton tonight on the wireless. Me and Jimmy heard him say that too. It was brilliant how it worked. When we got home dad joined the earphones together again. He said that they would be needed for the crystal set.

Mam said "It's a bit of a devil when your dad can find time to make you a telephone but can't find time to mend my iron. It

only needs a new element and you can buy one of those in Woolworths for half a crown".

Unknown to mam, dad gave me the half a crown before I went to bed. I have to call in Woolworths tomorrow to get the element. Dad says we must keep mam sweet. I don't quite understand what he means Maybe it's to do with S-E-X

13th June
Friday
Dear Diary   *Look at 9 on our map*

Today we decided to visit the horses at Kirkgate station stables. There are four horses and they are used to pull trucks in the railway sidings. Our Jimmy waited until mam went to hang out the washing, then pinched some carrots from the pantry. The horses love carrots. I called for Betty Smith, and Jimmy called for Dave Crosby. We then set off down Park Lodge Lane. As we passed the allotments we saw Betty's dad painting his shed. She asked him if he had any carrots to spare. He said he had, and pulled some up. When we poked our heads round the large stable door we could see only two horses there. My favourite horse is called Horace and our Jimmy's is called Percy. We don't know who gave them these names. Anyway, they weren't in the stables so we knew that they were working. We left the other two to feed the horses in the stable. We set off to find Horace and Percy. I found Horace pulling an empty truck towards a line of other trucks. An engine would come later to pull all the trucks away. Our Jimmy found Percy at the other end of the sidings. Percy was pulling a full truck of coal to where a lorry was waiting. We were not allowed down on the track while the trucks were being moved so we had to wait until the horses had finished. Then Bert, the man who looks after Horace, lifted me down so that I could feed Horace with the fresh carrots. Jimmy jumped down and fed Percy. When all the carrots had been eaten Bert led Horace to another truck. Percy was led back to the stables because he was limping badly. We went back to the stables with him. Fred, the head man, looked at Percy's legs and found that there was a nasty sore on one of them. He said it needed bathing straight away, and asked us to leave. As the four of us passed Betty's dad he called us across. He often wheeled his barrow to the stables to collect some manure, but he had a bad back. Could Jimmy and Dave fetch some for him? They set off, Dave wheeling the barrow, Jimmy sitting in it, holding the fork. What a funny sight. They returned a few minutes later, Jimmy wheeling the barrow piled high with manure.

Mam said "If you, our Jimmy, ever pinch my carrots again I'll make you eat cabbage for a month. And another thing, get into that bath immediately. You smell like the toilet when your dad's been. I'm sure you know what I mean".

Jimmy winked at me and smiled. We both knew that you had to wait at least ten minutes before going to the toilet after dad had been, especially if he'd had some beans. It smells like the sewage works down Turner's Lane.

26th June
Thursday
Dear Diary   *Look at 10 on our map*
The other day Bob, the lockkeeper down at the canal, showed us
his collection of clay pipes that he said the men called navvies had

smoked as they dug the canal. Bob said that the word navvy comes from the word navigation. He'd found the clay pipes in the sandy soil that the men had dug out to make the bank. Well today me, our Jimmy, Tom Crosby and May Williams decided to look for some pipes ourselves. Jimmy smuggled two garden trowels out of our shed. Dad would have killed him if he'd known. Anyway, off we went. We crossed King George playing field and headed down Park Lodge Lane towards the canal. Bob had told us that the best place to look was between the Red Bridge and the swing bridge, so we looked there. May and me looked where the bank was soft and we could use our hands. Jimmy and Tom dug deeper using the trowels. Tom was the first to find something. He found the bowl of a pipe. Then our Jimmy found part of a stem, about three inches long, with a hole all the way through it. As I dug into the soft sandy bank I found a bit of stem sticking up. As I removed more sand, more stem appeared. Then the sand surrounding the stem fell away revealing a perfect pipe. I carefully pick it up, rinsed it in the canal and dried it on my handkerchief. A little later May found an even better one. Hers had a curved stem, and had a face on the bowl. Jimmy and Tom were really jealous because, using their trowels, they had only managed to find bits and pieces of clay pipes. But that was better than nothing. As we made our way back towards the Red Bridge we saw Richard James and Alan Knott walking along the bank towards us. They asked us what we'd been doing. Like a fool, Jimmy told them, and showed them his bits of clay pipe. Tom did the same probably because he was frightened. May and me said nothing. We'd already carefully stuck our perfect pipes up our jumpers. Jamesy demanded the bits from the two lads and threw them in the canal. He and Knotty then walked away laughing. They are the most horrible lads on the estate. Nobody likes them. *Mam said "If that Richard James picks on you again, our Jimmy, I'm going to give his mother a right piece of my mind. And by the way, your dad's got those boxing gloves. He says it's about time you learned how to defend yourself".*

Everybody hopes that one day some lad will turn on Richard James and give him a good pasting, but I'm not sure that it will be our Jimmy. If it is, every kid on our estate will pat him on the back, all except Alan Knott, Jamesy's mate.

28th June
Saturday
Dear Diary *Look at 11 on our map*
This morning me and our Jimmy went to the Junior Club at the Empire cinema in Kirkgate. The doors open at quarter to ten but you have to be there before half past nine if you want a good seat. The show starts at ten. This morning we started with a singsong. The words are put up on the screen and a ball moves across the top of them so that you can keep in time. My favourite song is The Rio Grande, and we sang it this morning. Then a blind man called Francis Walker played some songs on his piano accordion. We sang to those too. The cartoons followed, with our favourite, Tom and Gerry. The serial always follows the cartoons, and the serial at the moment is Flash Gordon. He's been sent into space without his

34

oxygen supply. We have to wait until next week to see if he dies, but he won't. He never does. Finally we saw a Roy Rogers film, with his white horse Trigger. His ranch was attacked by oilmen who wanted his land, but Roy chased them away, and we all cheered. Trigger got shot but he soon got better. The film ended at twelve o'clock. May Williams and me walked slowly home but our Jimmy and Dave Crosby ran off, leaving us. It was only when I got home that I found out why. Jimmy was in our shed making a gun. He had cut a piece of pipe with a saw and was hammering it into a cotton reel that he had pinched from my mam's sewing basket. She'll go off the deep end when she finds out. He then shaped a piece of wood with my dad's penknife so that it looked like a gun handle. Finally he nailed the wood to the cotton reel and tapped in a nail for the trigger. He then pinched my dad's trilby and ran into the street, slapping his bum. He was now Roy Rogers, and he was on Trigger. As he ran he shot Mrs Burton's cat and Mr Craven's car tyres. He then ran into Trevor Collins who had also been to the Junior Club. Trev stuck a real gun in Jimmy's side. Well, not a real gun. It looks like a real gun but it only shoots caps, Trevor's mam had bought it for him on the market yesterday. Trev pulled the trigger and the cap banged, Jimmy dropped to the floor, dead. Well, not really dead. Jimmy then shot Trev but it wasn't the same because Jimmy had to shout BANG.

Mam said "Two weeks ago it was carrots. Today it was one of my cotton reels and your dad's hat. If you, our Jimmy, take another thing that doesn't belong to you I will take you to the police station myself and ask them to lock you up".

Poor Jimmy. Mam is always saying that she will get him locked up. Mind you, I wish she would, then I can have the big back bedroom with the big double bed.

5th July
Saturday
Dear Diary *Look at 12 on our map*

This morning we couldn't go to the Junior Club because mam said polio's about, and our Jimmy and me have to keep away from large groups of people. I asked if that also means school, but she

said No, Don't be so daft. I don't know what polio is but mam says that Johnny Moxon, who has calipers on his legs, had polio when he was younger. Anyway, we decided to go down to the weir because some of the lads had told our Jimmy that the river's very high after last week's heavy rain. I don't understand why the lads are attracted to the weir when the river is high so it was time to find out. Mam said we could only go if I kept an eye on our Jimmy. The walk along the length of Park Lodge Lane took about half an hour. We crossed the Red Bridge and cut across the field opposite Elliots Farm to the weir. Even though we were some distance away we could hear the roar of the fast flowing river. I saw some of Jimmy's mates on the bank only inches from the edge. He wanted to join them but I held him back. Mam would have killed me if he'd fallen in and drowned. Jimmy soon got bored and said he was going home. I was too, so we set off back. As we were crossing the Red Bridge we saw a coal train coming towards us from Newlands Pit. As it passed us our Jimmy, cheeky devil, asked the engine driver for a lift. To our surprise the driver stopped and told us to climb up onto the footplate. (our Jimmy told me that's its name). The driver started the train but told us to crouch down as we passed through Parkhills Pit. He said someone may be watching. When we were past we stood up and looked out. As we crossed Park Lodge Lane we saw Richard James and Alan Knott walking down. We waved and shouted but they ignored us because they were jealous. I bet we were the first kids on the whole of Eastmoor Estate to get a ride on a coal train. When we got to the pit yard the train stopped. We climbed down and ran behind a row of trucks so that we weren't seen. We cut across Gelder's field and were home in five minutes.

Mam said "Don't you ever ask the engine driver for a lift again. If you'd been seen in the pit yard he'd have got sacked, and you, our Jimmy would have been to blame. And you, our Jenny, being older, should have had more sense. Next time, think".

I suppose what mam said makes sense really, but it was still great. Wait until Jimmy tells his mates at school. They'll be real jealous, but what if the dad of one of them also works at the pit? If he says something he could get the engine driver sacked. I'd better warn him to keep his big mouth shut.

10th July
Thursday
Dear Diary   *Look at 13 on our map*
Today I did something that I'd never done before, and it proved just how brave I am. I'd certainly never seen a girl do it before. After tea our Jimmy and me walked up Parkgate Avenue to the rec. (dad says it's short for recreation, something to do with playing. I suppose it makes sense) Anyway, when we got there three of Jimmy's mates were playing tigs on the slide. Jimmy joined in straight away. I asked if I could but he said no. It was dangerous, and only for boys. I threatened to tell mam that he'd pinched a couple of candles out of the kitchen drawer to make the slide go faster by rubbing candle wax on it. She was getting fed up of his pinching.

He then changed his mind and said I could play but only if I was ON. I didn't mind that because I knew that I would soon tig someone. I decided to chase Denis Kelly first. He ran up the steps of the slide and I followed. I expected him to go down the slide, and I knew that I'd a good chance of tigging him there, but he

didn't. Instead he climbed over the top and slid down the posts. I didn't dare to follow so I had to go down the slide and chase someone else. Denis Kelly now got real cocky (is that cheeky?) and started to get onto me. I decided to chase him again.

Up the stairs he went, me after him. Again he climbed over the top and started to slide down the posts. This time I plucked up courage, climbed over the top and followed him. He didn't expect me to do this, and was too slow. As he reached the ground and ran away I stuck out my right leg and caught him on the head, tigging him. The other lads laughed at him for letting a girl tig him. He started to chase me to tig me back but Jimmy told him to pick on someone else. Anyway, he still chased me and I started to climb back up the slide. Since I had my gym pumps on I was able to grip the slippery surface even though our Jimmy had given it a good waxing. Denis Kelly had his leather boots on. He couldn't get a grip and kept sliding back down. The lads laughed at him again and I could see that he was getting real mad. He then started to chase Dave Crosby, but Dave was far too quick. He was the fastest up the stairs, up the slide and down the posts. I quite like Dave.

Mam said "It's bad enough having one monkey in the house (meaning our Jimmy) without my only daughter turning into one as well This house get more like a zoo every day, what with the antics of you two, and the rude noises your dad makes".

Our Jimmy ran round the living room, scratching under his arms and making monkey noises. And do you know what? He just looks like a monkey.

14th July
Saturday
Dear Diary   *Look at 14 on our map*
The other night our Jimmy and me went to the Kingfishers at Sun Lane Baths. Dad had made us members to get us swimming. Jimmy is now quite good. He has his GREEN for swimming a hundred yards. I've got my RED for swimming a length on my front and a length on my back. I'm going in for my GREEN next week. Anyway, when we were there Tom Crosby said that if it's sunny on Saturday (today) a big gang of kids is going swimming in the warm water pond down at Parkhills Pit. Our Jimmy told Tom that

he'd be going too. I said that I was as well, but he said I couldn't. It was only for boys. I had to threaten to tell mam that he intended to go, because she said it was dangerous down at the pit.

She would have stopped him. Jimmy therefore had to let me go with him.

This afternoon, just after dinner, we both secretly put on our swimming things under our clothes while our mam was putting out the washing. Jimmy even smuggled out a brand new white towel from the airing cupboard in his bedroom. Jimmy met up with Dave and Tom Crosby at the end of the street, and I asked Betty Smith if she wanted to come too. She did. We cut across the estate to Windhill Road and made our way to the warm water pond without being seen by the watchman. When we got there I counted four boys and a couple of girls swimming in the warm water. My dad says it's warm because it's pumped from the bottom of the pit where it's hot. But why? The cellar at Auntie May's house is underground and freezing cold, so why should a pit which is much deeper be hot? It doesn't make sense. Anyway, we put our clothes in a pile and our Jimmy dived in. I can't dive so I jumped. It was just like having a warm bath. at home. The water has a funny taste and is slightly brown in colour. Dad says it's due to the iron in the water. But it seems all right, and kids have been swimmiug there for ages without catching some terrible disease. We were really enjoying ourselves when we saw the watchman walking towards us. Everybody climbed out, grabbed their clothes and ran to the fence. No one got caught.

Mam said "I found a brand new white towel in the wash today, only it was the colour of stewed tea. If you, our Jimmy, don't wash your hands with soap in future I'm going to scrub them with VIM. I'll show you".

I'm hoping that she doesn't look in the airing cupboard. My costume and Jimmy's trunks are in there, drying. I hope they don't dry brown like stewed tea or she'll put two and two together, and work out where we've been. Then there'll be trouble.

18th July
Friday
Dear Diary   Look at 15 on our map

Most evenings our Jimmy and his mates go down to Kirkgate
Station on their bikes, trainspotting. Jimmy says that they go to see
the boat train because the engine is usually something special. I
can't understand why it's called a boat train. Dad explained. The
train comes from Newcastle and goes to Liverpool where it links
up with a boat that sails to Ireland. I suppose the name makes
sense. Anyway, this evening my best friend, Betty Smith, had to
stay in for cheeking Mrs Hunter who lives next door, Betty called
her an old bag, but I didn't manage to find out why, but I will
tomorrow. Being at a loose end I decided to follow Jimmy, Dave
and Tom Crosby down to the station. The best spot to see the
trains seems to be the top of a high wall overlooking the railway
sidings. When I caught up with them they were perched on it like
birds on a telephone wire. It seemed a bit dangerous because of
the long drop on the other side, but you know what lads are like.
My mam says that they can't see danger when it's staring them in

43

the face. Anyway, at exactly ten to eight the train came in. I only had a couple of seconds to see it, but I was able to see that the engine had a name just below the chimney. It was called - COCK O' THE NORTH. The three lads shouted "It's a cop. It's a cop." It seemed a daft thing to shout, so I asked our Jimmy why he was getting all excited. He told me that a cop is an engine you haven't seen before and this one is very rare. The lads then rode down to the station, got onto the platform through the parcels gate and moved towards the engine before the guard could stop them. Dave tried to reach up and touch the nameplate but it was far too high. He moved back, disappointed. Tom later told me that touching the nameplate is something really special. Then Jimmy darted up to the engine driver and said something to him. He then climbed onto the footplate and waved at Dave and Tom. They were real jealous of him because they said he'd cabbed the engine. Today I learned two things about trainspotting - copping and cabbing. No wonder lads are so daft.

Mam said "If I'd have been there I'd have asked the engine driver to keep you, our Jimmy, on the train until it got to Liverpool, and then put you on a slow boat to China. And

another thing, our Jenny. never say the word COCK. It's not very nice".

But she never tells us why we mustn't say certain words. And why is it that our dad is allowed to use them? Only the other day I heard him talking about ball cocks and stop cocks when the toilet started leaking.

20th July
Sunday
Dear Diary   *Look at 16 on our map*

Today I saw our Jimmy sneaking out of the shed with a large sack. I snatched it from him and looked inside. I found an axe, a saw, a hammer and some long nails. Dad would have gone mad if he'd seen them. Anyway, I asked Jimmy where he was going with them. He told me to mind my own business, so I threatened to tell mam about the sack. He soon changed his mind. He told me that he, Mick Peterson, and Dave and Tom Crosby were going down to Little Wood to build a tree house. I said I was coming too. He said I couldn't so I again threatened to tell mam. We walked the full

length of Park Lodge Lane then took the cart track to Little Wood. While our Jimmy was sawing branches off some trees, Dave and Tom were up the tree hammering nails into planks of wood that Mick and me had collected from the foot of the slag heap. Soon the tree house started to take shape. The floor and sides were made of planks, and the roof was made of branches covered with leaves. When it was finished it looked a bit like those houses you see in books on Africa at school. Our Jimmy, Dave and Tom found it easy to climb up to the tree house but I found it difficult. Maybe I was a bit scared. Mick therefore cut some strips of wood and nailed them up the trunk of the tree. As we sat there, looking out of the doorway (we didn't have enough wood to make a door) we saw Richard James and Alan Knott coming along the track. We kept quiet and still, and hoped that they wouldn't see us. But they did. We knew what would happen next because Jamesy was that sort of lad. Both climbed up and started to throw the roof branches down to the ground. Then Knotty started to kick the sides in. The five of us had to scramble down the trunk and look on helplessly. When our tree house was completely smashed, Jamesy and Knotty walked away, laughing.

Mam said *"There are people in this world who always want to spoil things for others. It's a hard fact of life. But never be put off by them. And by the way, our Jimmy, how did you manage to build a tree house without any tools?"*

The five of us decided there and then to return to Little Wood in the morning and rebuild the tree house. Of course, it will mean our Jimmy smuggling the sack of tools out of the shed again, The trouble is, mam will be watching him like a hawk because I think she suspects that all wasn't above board this morning. But this time I'll be helping him by trying to distract her. Maybe I'll ask her to give me that talk on S-E-X. That should do the trick.

31st July
Thursday
Dear Diary   Look at 17 on our map
We built our best den ever today. Me, my friend Betty Smith, our Jimmy and his mate Mick Peterson found a big elderberry bush in the hedge that separates Gelder's Field from Park Lodge Lane.

Mick managed to climb straight into the bush from the top of the bank on the Lane but couldn't climb down because the bush was too thick. Jimmy ran back home and returned with an axe and a saw. He seems to use dad's tools more than dad does. At least that's what my mam says. She's been waiting weeks for dad to box in the bath. Anyway, Jimmy returned and climbed into the top of the bush and started to hack through the upper branches. Soon he was able to climb down to the bottom. He then told the three of us to follow. Mick went first, then me, and finally Betty. We now found ourselves in a den with a thick roof of leaves, and about ten feet below Park Lodge Lane. Then Mick had a great idea. On our way to Gelder's Field he'd seen a piece of rubber belt about eight feet long and two feet wide just outside the pit yard gate. Jimmy says rubber belts are used to carry coal from the trucks to the chutes that fill the lorries. Jimmy again ran home and this time returned with a hammer and four long nails. At the same time he collected the piece of belting. With our help he nailed one end of the belt to a branch at the top and the other end to a branch near the bottom. We could then climb into the bush at the top of the

48

bank and slide down the belt into our den at the bottom. Mick tried to climb back up but couldn't. In order to get to the top again we had to scramble back up the steep bank. The four of us agreed that on the next rainy day we would go to the den just to see if it is waterproof. I bet it is. It is now important to keep our den a secret. We know that if Richard James and Alan Knott find it they will wreck it just like they did to our tree house the other day.

Mam said "Don't ever take your dad's tools out of the shed again, our Jimmy. If you lose them it just gives him an excuse not to get on with boxing my bath in. I've only been waiting six months".

Our Jimmy is always taking my dad's tools out of the shed. The trouble is he has the bad habit of losing them. I know for certain that he left a big hammer down at Little Wood the other day. On the way home I'd offered to carry the sack of tools, and the hammer wasn't in it. Jimmy said that it must have fallen out while I was carrying the sack. He tried to blame me, but I think he'd left it at the foot of the tree.

10th August
Sunday
Dear Diary   Look at 18 on our map
My dad will kill our Jimmy if he finds out what he's done today.
Dave Crosby and Mick Peterson called for him to come out and
play Peggy. Let me explain what Peggy is. The Peggy is a small
piece of wood about four inches long and sharpened to a point at
both ends with a knife. It is placed on the ground and the sharp
point is struck with a stick. The Peggy jumps up in the air and is hit
with the stick. The person who hits it the furthest is the winner.
Mick and Dave only had a thin cane to hit the Peggy so our Jimmy
pinched dad's walking stick from the shed. Dad uses it to help him
to walk when his bad knee gives him some gyp. Jimmy shortened
it by sawing off the curved handle. He then tried it on the Peggy. It
was perfect, and soon all three lads were hitting the Peggy miles.
Unfortunately Mick knocked it into Mrs Smith's front garden, and
she wouldn't let them have it back. The three then decided to play
Sticks. Let me now explain how you play Sticks. Two pieces of
wood six inches long are propped up against a wall or kerb. Another

piece of wood of the same size is carefully balanced across the top of the other two. The idea of the game is to throw a tennis ball at the sticks from a distance of about ten feet. If it hits the sticks the thrower runs away and the others have to chase him passing the ball as they chase. When the chance arises the chasers try to hit the thrower with the ball. If they succeed the thrower is OUT. But if the thrower can get back to the sticks and set them up again before being hit he has another throw at them. Otherwise a new thrower aims at the sticks. If there are enough players two teams are picked – the throwers and the chasers. When all the throwers are OUT, the chasers become the throwers and the game continues. Since the lads did not have any sticks our Jimmy sawed the walking stick (now without a curved handle) into three six inch lengths. The game then started.

Mam said "When your dad's knee starts giving him some gyp in future, our Jimmy you will do all the gardening, all the grass cutting and all the coal fetching and anything else I can think of. I'll show you.... You little vandal".

A Peggy

51

Luckily for our Jimmy, dad's knee was okay for weeks and weeks. But one day he hurt it getting off his bike and went looking for his walking stick. When he couldn't find it he asked our Jimmy if he knew where it was. The little liar told him that he could remember him leaving it at Eastmoor Working Men's Club after a game of bowls a few weeks ago. Someone must have pinched it.

18th August
Monday
Dear Diary   *Look at 19 on our map*
There is a lad up our street called Tony Steel. He is eighteen and a right good swimmer. He works at Sun Lane Baths and swims for the Kingfishers. The other day our Jimmy was talking to him and he said that he was going to swim the Channel next year. Jimmy told dad and he said that pigs might fly. Tony said that he trains in the sand quarry on the other side of the canal every evening after work. He says he swims five miles a day. Dad said he was pulling our leg. Anyway, today our Jimmy suggested that we went down

to the sand quarry to see Tony training. Just after tea we sneaked upstairs and put on our swimming things under our clothes. Jimmy then tried to smuggle a towel out of the house, but mam caught him. He told her that it had fallen off the line and he was just pegging it back up. I could tell that she didn't believe him. It took us about half an hour to reach the sand quarry. As we walked onto a sandy beach Tony swam towards us, and he looked like a channel swimmer too, with his goggles on. We asked if we could swim a few yards with him and he said yes as long as we could still touch the bottom. But we were soon out our depth and he sent us back to the beach. We were disappointed but I knew that it was the right thing to do. Besides, if our Jimmy had drowned my mam would have killed me. Of course, if I'd drowned she'd have killed him. I found it strange, swimming in the water. It was quite warm on the top but freezing cold a couple of feet down, but much worse, you couldn't see the bottom. Up until now I have only swum at Sun Lane Baths, where you can always see the bottom and you always know how deep the water is. As Tony swam to the other side he got smaller and smaller, and almost disappeared. He then swam back. As he did so Jimmy and me dried ourselves on Tony's towel. Jimmy then went behind a bush and put his clothes on. I wasn't going to do that so I had to put my clothes on over my wet costume. It felt really awful. Tony's towel was wet and sandy but he didn't complain. He just slipped on his tracksuit. We then started the long walk home.

Mam said "I've just this minute found a wet pair of trunks and a wet swimming costume in my oven. Any ideas how they got there, our Jenny, since I only washed and dried them the other day?"

Our Jimmy had the answer. He told her that he'd just finished having a bath when he decided to get the swimming things ready for Tuesday's swimming club. He said he accidently dropped them in the water. Mam didn't believe a word.

20th August
Wednesday
Dear Diary   *Look at 20 on our map*
Devil's Hollow (we say Holla) is like an island in the middle of the
cornfield opposite Gelder's Field. It is covered with hawthorn,

elderberry, long grass and bracken. No one knows why it's called Devil's Hollow, but me and Jimmy have been there when it's coming in dark, and it's a real spooky place. So maybe that's the reason. Anyway, this evening me, my friend Betty Smith, our Jimmy and his mates Mick Peterson, and Dave and Tom Crosby went there to play hide and seek. Since the corn had just been cut and the field was ready for ploughing we didn't think we'd be trespassing, walking across it, but we didn't really know. So as not to be in too much trouble we walked down Turner's Lane and ran the short distance across the field to the Hollow. Dave picked up a piece of straw and broke it into six. We then drew a straw each. I drew the shortest so I was ON first. I counted up to thirty, then shouted READY OR NOT. No sooner had I started looking for the others when I saw a tractor, pulling a plough, enter the field through the gate by the hospital. The others came out of their hiding places, and we all crouched down and moved towards the middle where the farmer couldn't see us. We were trapped, and it was already becoming dusk. If we didn't escape anything could happen to us. Jimmy guessed that it was about half past eight, and we had to be in by nine. Then Dave had a great idea. If we waited until the farmer was on the opposite side of the Hollow to Turner's Lane he would not be able to see us as we ran across the field and made our escape. So that's what we decided to do. But the tractor took ages to go round the field and behind the bushes.

Then it did and we ran as fast as we could towards the fence on Turner's Lane and the cover of the trees. We'd made it. We then ran up the lane and headed for home as fast as we could. As the farmer came round the back of the Hollow he looked across and waved. Had he seen us? I bet he had. As we rushed through the back door, out of breath, mam pointed to the clock on the kitchen wall. It showed exactly five past nine. She wasn't best pleased. *Mam said "Why the guilty looks on your faces, you two? Anybody would think that you'd been up to no good. Have*

you? And another thing. You're six minutes late. You were meant to be in by nine, at the latest".

Jimmy said, "Only five minutes late mam, not six." He then ducked as she tried to clip him round the ear, She missed. Mind you, that wasn't surprising since our Jimmy has had a lot of practice at avoiding mam's clips round the ear.

21st August
Thursday
Dear Diary *Look at 21 on our map*
This morning me and our Jimmy were at a loose end so we called for Dave and Tom Crosby, but Mrs Crosby said they were already out playing so we headed up Park Lodge Lane looking for them. But we didn't find them. Jimmy then remembered that every morning a coal train comes up the line next to Turner's Lane and reverses back into Parkhills Pit. So we headed down the lane and were just in time. We could see the train in the distance coming towards us. By the fence and only a couple of yards from the line there's a thick elderberry bush. We decided to crouch down behind it just

before the engine reached the buffers. The engine stopped and the driver climbed down and walked to the end of the row of trucks in order to change the points. When he returned and started to climb up onto the footplate our Jimmy whistled at him. The driver looked across but could not see us. He disappeared into the cab. Jimmy whistled again. The driver looked out. He knew that someone was playing a game with him, but he still couldn't see us. He then shouted across in our direction. "So you think you can whistle, do you? Well listen to mine." At that he reached up and pulled something inside the cab. The engine's whistle blasted and steam shot straight up in the air. Because we were so near, the noise was deafening. As he started to reverse his engine, me and Jimmy moved into the open so the driver could see us. We waved and he waved back. It was then that we realized that it was Mr Kelly, Denis's dad, who lives at the top of our street. His face was black but we could still tell it was him. He stopped the train and waved us down. This meant climbing over the fence and trespassing, but Mr Atkinson had waved us down so it was all right. He then told us to climb up into the cab. I wanted to blow the whistle so he let me. Jimmy wanted to shovel some coal into the fire. Mr Atkinson was quite happy to let him do that. I thought about telling him that we'd once had a ride on an engine, but decided not to. I didn't want to get the other driver into trouble.

Mam said "I hope you didn't give Mr Kelly any cheek, because if you did I'll get to know. His wife works with me at the hospital, and I'm not having you two being cheeky to one of the neighbours, so there".

Jimmy said that we were very polite, which of course we were, but mam said that he doesn't know the meaning of the word. Mind you, our Jimmy doesn't know the meaning of a lot of words. Mam says he was at the back of the queue when God gave the brains out.

15th September
Monday
Dear Diary *Look at 22 on our map*
I have now become a trainspotter, well not really. It's because my

mam wants me to keep an eye on our Jimmy who's as daft as a brush. Why a brush I wonder? Why should a brush be classed as daft? Anyway, this evening Jimmy, Dave Crosby and Mick Peterson went on their bikes to get the boat train. I tagged along on Betty Smith's bike. Her mam said I could borrow it because Betty has mumps. I hope I can't get mumps from the handlebars. Jimmy and his mates then decided to go to the Ninety Nine Arches to see the Yorkshire Pullman. Jimmy told me that this is a train that goes to Leeds from London, and passes over the arches at quarter to nine. It was already getting dark but we have lights on our bikes. Mick had his dad's wrist watch with him and at exactly quarter to nine the train was pegged (this means that the signal goes up to show that the train is coming). In the distance we heard a train whistle sound. All the lads shouted "A STREAK A STREAK." I had not heard the word before to do with trains but I knew that my mam sometimes bought streaky bacon at Jowett's butchers. Our Jimmy told me that a streak is a streamlined engine and one is pulling the train. They were very rare in Wakefield. Dave Crsoby then realized that it was too dark to see the number of the engine. They would not know which streak it was. Our Jimmy had the answer. He quickly turned his bike upside down, clicked on the dynamo and told Dave to pedal right fast. He then tilted the front light so that the beam of light shone on the top of the arches. As the train passed he pointed the light onto the engine. Mick shouted "4468 - It's MALLARD. It's MALLARD. The lads cheered because it was another cop. I cheered as well. I don't quite know why, but I did. I then looked at Dave's watch in the light. It was ten to nine. Jimmy and I had to be in for nine. We knew that mam would go off the deep end when we got home, and she did too.

Mam said "If our Jimmy is going to treat his bike like a piece of junk, then I'm going to tell his dad to advertise it in Price's paper shop window. Hopefully it will go to some nice child who will really appreciate it. Or he can give it to little Johnny Smales. You know, that poor little lad who lives with his grandma".

Our Jimmy put his arm round her and started to cry. I think he was pretending. So did she. She pushed him away and told him that he couldn't get round her that way. He has to mend his ways, But how do you mend ways? You can mend shoes. My dad is always mending his, but I've never seen him mend his ways.

16th September
Tuesday
Dear Diary   *Look at 23 on our map*
Today straight after tea we went conkering. At school yesterday the lads had been playing conkers at playtime. Our Jimmy wanted to join in but he hadn't one. All the conker trees round here are in the grounds of the Mental Hospital where our dad works as a nurse, so we had to be careful. Dave and Tom Crosby came with us as we cut across the estate to Stanley Road and to the hospital grounds. We now met our first problem. The hospital is surrounded by iron railings ten feet high. Dad says it's to keep the patients in

and people like our Jimmy out. But just near the conker trees the railings had been pushed slightly apart. Our Jimmy, Dave and Tom managed to squeeze through but my thick hair made my head too big. Anyway, Tom had been conkering before and already had a big stick in his hand which he threw up in the air at the branches.

As the conkers fell Dave and Jimmy collected them up and passed them through the railings to me to stuff in a bag. Then we saw a man coming towards us. Dave quickly climbed through the railings followed by Tom, but our Jimmy was too slow and the man caught him. As it happened the man was Mr Sellers, one of my dad's work mates. He held Jimmy tightly and said that he would tell dad that we'd been trespassing in the hospital grounds. He then let Jimmy go. When we got home we peeled off the outer casings and shared the conkers out. Dave and Tom had heard that baking them in the oven made them hard and last longer in a conker fight, so that's what they did. My dad had told our Jimmy that he used to soak them in vinegar, so Jimmy decided to try that. I threaded mine on a string, all except five. I polished these with some of mam's brown polish and put them on the dressing table in my bedroom. I didn't keep my conkers long, however. Our Jimmy pinched them and put them in the oven. He said that the vinegar method would take ages to work.

Mam said "Don't you two expect me to defend you when your dad comes home from work and gives you a good telling off for trespassing. I won't. And another thing, our Jimmy. You've pinched nearly all the vinegar. You can go without tonight when your sister fetches the fish and chips. Don't put any vinegar on his at the fish shop, our Jenny, even if he asks you to".

Jimmy loves fish and chips. He loves them even better when they have lots of vinegar on them. Unknown to mam he sneaked upstairs, raided his piggy bank and gave me a sixpence to get some vinegar from Parker's off licence. Since I like lots of vinegar on mine as well I agreed to get a bottle, and we'd hide it from mam by keeping it in the shed.

24th September
Wednesday
Dear Diary   *Look at 24 on our map*
We had just finished our tea when Betty Smith and her brother

Keith called for us. It was already getting dark and mam told us that we could play out till eight o'clock but we couldn't go out of the street. We therefore decided to play hide and seek under the street lights. It wasn't long before Dave and Tom Crosby came out and joined in. Then Keith said that he had something to show

us but it would mean us going out of the street. Our Jimmy was all for going. I didn't want to because of what mam had said, but she had also said on many occasions that we must always stick together, so I decided to go. Keith then disappeared and returned with a torch that he had taken from his dad's shed. We headed up Park Lodge Lane and into the road that leads to the County hospital. Keith led us to a place that was divided up by walls about six feet high. It was really spooky because Keith's torch made long shadows of everything. He then told us to stay where we were while he disappeared behind a wall. He took the torch with him, me and Betty were really frightened. I bet the lads were too but they said they weren't. Anyway, we then heard a sort of moaning sound and a beam of light shone above the wall. This was even more frightening. As we stared at the beam an arm appeared above the wall, then another, then a leg, then another leg. They obviously weren't Keith's unless he was standing on his hands on a box. The arms and legs disappeared and the beam went out. It was now pitch black and even the lads were frightened. We whispered to Keith to switch on the torch, which he did. Then something fell from the sky. It was a leg. I screamed. Then an arm fell. Betty screamed. In the dim light our Jimmy bravely reached out and touched the leg. "It's made of rubber. It's made of rubber," he shouted. He then picked it up. Keith appeared with a couple of arms in his hands. and said that they were artificial limbs, like the ones a person without legs or arms has to have. They had been dumped there. As we walked back home we decided to call the place THE TOMBS. We hoped that one day we would find a mummy there, you know, like the ones you see in the books on ancient Egypt at school.

Mam said "Don't you ever go near that hospital again. You may pick up a terrible disease that eats your body away. Now both of you go and get in the bath. You first, our Jenny. Your brother can use the water after you".

Our Jimmy started to scratch his knee. He rolled up his trouser leg, and there was a red patch on his kneecap. Was the dreaded disease already starting to eat his knee away?

27th September
Saturday
Dear Diary   *Look at 25 on our map*
I caught our Jimmy acting strangely today. On our way home from the Junior Club he found a sheet of metal outside the foundry on Peterson Road. It was about six feet long., and he struggled to carry it home. He went into the shed and closed the door. I looked through the window to see what he was doing. He was cutting the sheet in half with what looked like a big pair of scissors, but they weren't. I'd seen dad using them before to cut a piece of metal from a treacle tin. Jimmy came out of the shed with two pieces of metal sheet. Both were curved up at one end. After dinner he sneaked into the living room and removed mam's gloves from the sideboard drawer. He then picked up his sheets and called for Dave and Tom Crosby, and Denis Kelly. They also had some

gloves. I called for Betty Smith and told her that Jimmy and his mates were up to something, and that we should follow them. They headed across King George playing field, down Park Lodge Lane and along the canal bank to Parkhills pit. Me and Betty followed close behind. The lads knew we were there but didn't bother. We climbed to the top of the pit heap and all was revealed why Jimmy had brought his metal sheets. He placed one of them at the top of the steep slope and sat on it, placing his feet behind the curve. He then edged forward and shot down the slope to the bottom at high speed. Dave followed on the other sheet. The two lads carried the sheets back up the slope so that Tom and Denis could have a go, Tom shot down to the bottom followed by Denis. Then it was our turn, but we fell off about half way down. I tore my trousers on a sharp stone and Betty rubbed a big hole in the elbow of her jumper. I knew that we'd both be in trouble when we got home. The lads soon got fed up of carrying the sheets back up the slope so Jimmy hid them in the hedge bottom. They could be used again later. As we walked back home me and Betty tried to come up with an explanation for the damage to our clothes. Was there some way I could put the blame on our Jimmy?

Mam said "Now, our Jenny. How in heaven's name did you come to tear your best trousers? I told you not to wear them if you were playing out with your daft brother. So what were you doing then? Let's have it".

I told her that the number plate on Mr Craven's car has a sharp corner, and I caught my trouser leg on it when Jimmy chased me up the street. It was therefore all his fault, not mine. Mam glared at me, then at our Jimmy. She didn't believe a word. She hasn't found her torn gloves yet.

10th October
Friday
Dear Diary   *Look at 26 on our map*

Last night we went for the first time to the Carlton cinema. We usually go to the Empire, Regal and Playhouse, but not to the Carlton because mam says it's not the sort of place nice people go to. She didn't explain why. Anyway, Robin Hood was on and our

Jimmy wanted to see it. He likes films where there's a lot of fighting. I don't, but mam said he could only go if I went with him. Dave and Tom Crosby went with us. We had to go nearly into town to get there because mam said we couldn't use the short cut down the station yard to the bottom of Kirkgate because it was dark. When we reached the cinema there was a bit of a queue but the

usherette soon showed us to our seats. We were sat near the back but we could still see quite well. The lights went out and the film started, but soon I heard strange sounds coming from the back row. When I turned round I saw that the seats were double seats, and the noises were coming from couples kissing and cuddling. I couldn't understand why they'd come to the cinema at all. It was certainly not to see the film. The three lads thought the film was great and they wished that they'd lived at the same time as Robin Hood, but they wouldn't have liked sleeping on a straw bed or washing in a cold stream. Mind you, our Jimmy doesn't get washed at all if he can help it. And he'd have had to go to the toilet behind a bush, but he sometimes does that when he's playing out, so his mates told me. Mam would go kill him if she knew. All today the lads have been making swords and bows and arrows from bits of wood and canes from my dad's raspberry patch. There'll be trouble when he finds out. They then started fighting with the swords and shooting arrows at my dad's long johns on the washing line. Mam wasn't best pleased and took the bows and arrows off the lads. She cut the bowstrings with some scissors and stuck the arrows back in the raspberry patch She also reminded them that only last year Joan Frost had lost an eye having been hit in the face by an arrow.

Mam said "If you go to the Carlton again, our Jenny, I don't want you looking round at those people on the back row to see what they're up to. And I definitely don't want to hear that you've been sitting on the back row yourself. Right?"

I hope our Jimmy doesn't tell her that Dave Crosby has asked me to go with him next week to the Carlton to see a film called Cloak and Dagger. I don't know what I'll do if he wants us to sit on the back row. I suppose I'll say yes, but what if one of the neighbours sees us? Mam will kill me.

22nd October
Wednesday
Dear Diary   *Look at 27 on our map*

During half term most of the kids on our estate go potato picking. Me and our Jimmy decided to go this morning. You have to provide your own bucket. Mam has only one so I asked Mrs Craven, next door, if I could borrow hers. She said yes. I then called for Betty Smith. She was already waiting for me with her bucket. The potato fields are down near Parkhills pit so we set off at nine o'clock. As we walked across King George playing field Dave and Tom Crosby joined us. When we got to the fields lots of our friends were already there, all picking potatoes. A tractor pulls a sort of plough that brings the potatoes to the top. You then pick them up and put them in your bucket. Big ones are best because they fill up the bucket the quickest. You then take your full bucket to a man with a weighing scale. He empties your bucket, weighs the potatoes and puts them in a sack. He then gives you some money depending on the weight. The four of us got behind the tractor and some really big potatoes came up. We quickly filled our buckets but they were now very heavy. Me and Betty struggled to carry one. Even our Jimmy struggled with his. Before long my back started to ache with all the bending, and my arm felt as if it was coming out of its socket. I was also feeling very hungry so Joe asked a man what time it was. He said twelve o'clock. We decided that we'd done enough potato picking, and set off for home. After dinner Tom and Dave called for Jimmy. They said they were going back to the potato fields. Jimmy said he wasn't because his legs felt like jelly. A little bit later me and Jimmy went out on the street. Up at the top we saw Tom, Dave and some more mates playing with a rugby ball. They too had had enough potato picking. Jimmy said they were playing touch and pass, and he joined in. I called for Betty and we counted our money. We both had two and six each. I know what I'm going to do with mine. I am going to buy The Castle of Adventure by Enid Blyton. She's my favourite author. Betty says she's saving up for some new shoes.

Mam said "I've no sympathy with you two. No sympathy at all. Now you know how I feel when I'm carrying the potatoes,

groceries and bottles of pop from town. My back aches and my legs feel like jelly but I have to keep going otherwise you'd both starve. But do I get any sympathy? Do I hell".

Mam must be really mad, because she swore at us. She hates swearing and our Jimmy gets into real trouble when he loses his temper and swears. But we sometimes hear dad swear, especially when he hits his thumb with a hammer.

23rd October
Thursday
Dear Diary   *Look at 28 on our map*

Me and our Jimmy were at a loose end this morning. Dave and Tom had gone to town with their mam. Betty Smith had to stay in for cheeking Mrs Kent who lives at number one. It seems that Betty had been playing sticks with her brother Keith and a couple of his mates. She threw the ball at Keith but he ducked and the ball hit Mrs Kent's front window. The window didn't break but Mrs Kent wouldn't let them have the ball back. Betty called her an old bag. Her mam went mad when she heard about it. Anyway, me and Jimmy decided to head for the canal. Maybe we could get a lift in a sand lorry, or on the footplate of an engine. Maybe even a lift on a barge. That would be really great. As we looked towards the locks we saw a fully loaded barge waiting to pass through. We knew it was fully loaded because it was very low in the water. In fact we thought it was going to sink. Anyway, we ran to the locks and helped Bob the lockkeeper to push open the gates. The barge then passed through and pulled over to the bank. The man on it threw a rope to our Jimmy and told him to tie it to a large iron ring that was fastened to the canal wall. The man then jumped off and went for a cup of tea with Bob. We decided to have another look at Bob's collection of claypipes. He had found another one only last week. It has a face with a beard on the bowl and a fancy curved stem. Jimmy put it in his mouth and pretended to smoke it. When the man got back on his barge he shouted across to us, "Do you want a lift up to the swing bridge at Stanley Ferry?" We couldn't believe our luck. We jumped on and the man set off. As we passed under the Red Bridge we waved to Alan Knott and Richard James who were leaning over the rail. They didn't wave back, probably because they were jealous. The kids who live on the estate are always asking for lifts on the barges, but only two or three have ever managed it because the bargemen are too mean. We were lucky. Very lucky.

Mam said "What have I told you about accepting lifts from strange men, especially you our Jenny, even if it is on a barge? The man could have kidnapped you and taken you to Goole. How would you have got back then? Swim?"

Jimmy nudged me and whispered "Easy. It's only a few miles." I went to the bookcase, got out the atlas and turned to a map of Yorkshire. I measured the distance with a ruler, trying to follow the curves on the canal. I then converted it to miles using the scale. The distance came to about thirty five miles. Our Jimmy wouldn't have even got round the first bend.

5th November
Wednesday
Dear Diary

Look at 29 on our map

During dinnertime today we rushed home to build our bonfire. Our

Jimmy and his mates Dave and Tom Crosby, and Mick Peterson have been chubbing for weeks and all the wood they've collected is in our sheds to stop it being pinched by Richard James and his gang. They'd raided us two nights ago but got nothing. Last night was mischief night and we knew that Jamesy would be on the estate causing trouble, so Jimmy and Dave crept round to his house and pinched a couple of long planks from the back garden. We always have our bonfire on the small field between our street and Woodhouse road. To get to it we have to cut through Mr Whitworth's back garden. He doesn't mind as long as we stick to the path. It took us about an hour to build the bonfire, then we ran back to school. After tea we rushed back with our fireworks and some large potatoes that our Jimmy had pinched from the pantry. I sneaked some matches out of our house and gave them to Tom. He lit the newspaper that he'd placed under the wood. In no time at all the flames were the height of a house. It was now time to light our fireworks but first Dave lit a length of rope about six inches long. He called it TOUCH but didn't know why. The lads only had bangers and jumping jacks. Me and Betty had a box of roman candles, some golden rains and a couple of Catherine wheels. In no time at all the lads' fireworks had gone up in smoke. They then wanted to light ours. That was OK by us because we were a bit frightened. We had one rocket between us. Dave had saved some money from his paper round and bought it at Price's paper shop. He stood it in a milk bottle, lit it and stepped quickly back. Whoosh - up it went. It then banged but there were no stars. We saw the stick bounce off Mrs Hunter's roof. When the flames had died down we pushed our potatoes into the red hot ashes with a long stick. It took ages for them to do. When we tried them they were still hard and tasted horrible. Not long afterwards my dad came across the field and told us it was time we were in. I didn't mind really. I was hot, my clothes were dirty and my hair smelt of smoke. I looked a real mess. All I wanted was a good bath.

Mam said "You look as if you've been pulled through a hedge backwards, our Jenny. For goodness sake, you're not a boy, you're a girl. Well act like one, damn it".

She said nothing to our Jimmy. Mind you she's used to seeing him looking as black as the fire back. When he tried to sneak upstairs without having a bath she dragged him back and pulled down his underpants. His face was a picture

15th November

Saturday

Dear Diary   *Look at 30 on our map*

This morning dad built our Jimmy a crystal set. For those who don't know, a crystal set is made of a crystal, I don't know what sort, a cat's whisker, which isn't a cat's whisker really. It's a thin piece of wire that is scraped over the crystal to make it work.

It also has a coil of wire, something with a knob that turns, and some earphones. But it doesn't need a battery. Dad connected all the bits together but when he put on the earphones, scraped the crystal with the cat's whisker and turned the knob he couldn't hear

anything. He said it needed an earth wire connected to a water pipe. Our Jimmy's bedroom doesn't have one but mine does, so dad placed the crystal set on the little table in my room. This made Jimmy really mad. Dad tried again but he still couldn't hear anything. He said it also needed a long piece of wire as high up as possible. He called this the aerial. We needed a long pole. Jimmy knew where he could get one. Just off Park Lodge Lane, opposite King George playing field, they are building the new Spooner houses. Jimmy said he'd seen a pole there but it was bent. Anyway, this afternoon we walked up to the building site and asked the watchman if we could have the bent pole. To our surprise he said yes, so we carried it back home on our shoulders. When dad saw it he told us to grip the ends while he stood in the middle and jumped on it. After a few jumps the pole was almost straight. He then went into the shed and came out with a big coil of wire. He ran upstairs and connected one end to the crystal set and threw the rest of the wire out of the bedroom window. He then told us to tie the wire to one end of the pole while he dug a deep hole at the bottom of the garden. He stood the pole in the hole then filled it in with stones.

Me and Jimmy ran upstairs and he put the earphones on. He smiled. He said he could hear music. I then put the earphones on and I could hear a man talking. The crystal set worked. It is now dark and it works even better. Dad says that we may be able to pick up some foreign stations later.

Mam said "That's just typical of your father. He can spend all day making you a crystal set but can't find time to put me a shelf up in the kitchen. I've only been waiting six months for one".

Jimmy said that he'd put it up, and went to the shed. He returned with a hammer and some nails. He was about to knock a six-inch nail into the kitchen wall when dad stopped him. Dad then put up the shelf. Mam just smiled. She had shamed him into doing it, with a little help from our Jimmy, of course.

31st November
Friday
Dear Diary *Look at 31 on our map*
This evening our Jimmy did something really bad. I am ashamed to

call him my brother. And he told me he was pleased with himself for doing it too. What he and Dave Crosby did made it dangerous for anyone walking into town along Park Lodge Lane at night. Along the lower end of the lane there are gas lamps spaced out at intervals of about fifty yards. Every evening, just before it gets dark, a man called the lamp lighter goes along the lane lighting the lamps. He does this with a long pole that has a flame in the end of it. Why it doesn't blow out on a windy night I don't know, but it doesn't. First he turns the gas on by pushing open the tap just below the lamp with the pole. He then pushes the end of the pole into the lamp and lights the gas. Although I've never seen him, he must turn them off early in the morning. Anyway, our Jimmy and Dave went down Park Lodge Lane after all the lamps had been lit. As they came to each one either Jimmy or Dave shinned up the lamp post and turned it off by turning the tap. I know just how dark the lane is when all the lamps are out. I once had to go down to Parker's off licence for my mam some butter. It was really scary and I'm sure I saw a ghost as I ran past Goodair's Ginnel. It was all right for Jimmy and Dave because they were on their bikes and they have lights. It was a good job that the local bobby hadn't seen them. He'd have grabbed them, clipped them round the ear then marched them home. Dad would have given our Jimmy a good hiding and I know that Mr Crosby would have done the same to Dave. When Jimmy told me I was tempted to split on him to mam for being so silly, but didn't because he knew that I'd stolen a dog biscuit from a sack outside Halstead's grocery store. I only wanted to see what it tasted like. It wasn't very nice and I gave it to Mrs Craven's dog, Rover. He seemed to like it, but there again, he is a

dog and it was a dog biscuit. Anyway, our Jimmy said that if I didn't tell mam about him turning off the gas lamps he wouldn't tell her about me stealing a dog biscuit. I had to agree even though I thought that he was a bigger criminal than me.

Mam said "I've just been down to Warrengate fish shop to get the supper and I saw someone turning off all the gas lamps. Who ever it was needs a real good thrashing. I don't suppose you know anything about it do you, our Jimmy?"

I whispered to Jimmy, "I'm going to tell her it was you." He whispered back "If you do I'll tell her you're a thief." I said nothing, so he said nothing, but I hope that somebody saw him and tells her. I've never seen our Jimmy being thrashed.

25th December
Thursday
Dear Diary   *Look at 32 on our map*
Today is Christmas Day. Our Jimmy and me were up early to open our presents even though we already knew what they were. I had been promised a new bike because I had done really well at school. Mam had told Jimmy that if he was really good he may get a train set. When we walked into the living room there was this funny shaped parcel propped up against the wall and a large oblong parcel on the floor. Mam had tried hard to cover the bike with christmas paper but the handlebars, seat and pedals were showing. As I tore off the paper I could see that it was just what I wanted. It was a Raleigh, with cable brakes, Sturmer Archer three speed gears and a hub dynamo. I know about such things because our Jimmy has a

Raleigh and he's always going on about it. As I was unwrapping my parcel our Jimmy was unwrapping his. As he took off the paper we could see that it was an old suitcase. He was really disappointed. He slowly opened the two catches and lifted the lid. His eyes lit up. Inside was a train set, a Hornby and quite big. The engine is about eight inches long, painted green and has six wheels. There are also four trucks and two carriages, and lots of track. I helped him to fit the lines together on the carpet and soon we had a big layout (I think that's the right word). Jimmy wound up the engine with a big key and put it on the lines. We connected the trucks and carriages to it. He then pulled a little knob and the train started to move. It went round about four times before it needed winding up again. But Jimmy soon lost interest, watching it go round, and when I started to push my bike through the front door he helped me. When we got onto the road he asked if he could have first go. I said no, and set off up our avenue to the top. I then came back, changing gear all the time. It was the best present I've ever had. I felt mean not letting him have a go because I'd rode his bike many times even though it has a cross bar. So I let him have a go. As he pedalled

off I gasped because he nearly ran into the back of Mr Craven's
car.

*Mam said "Just watch our Jimmy with your new bike will
you, our Jenny? Given half the chance he'll turn the handlebars
upside down, turn the saddle round and stick transfers all over
it. He'll make it into a track bike, just like his own".*

There is only one thing I can do to stop him. When Halfords opens
on Monday I am going to buy a combination lock and chain so that
I can lock my bike up every time I put it in the shed. Mind you, it
wouldn't surprise me if Jimmy breaks the combination. He seems
to be good at that sort of thing. Maybe it's because he's good at
sums.

A final word from the author

Now that you have read some of the entries from Jenny's diary I hope that you will be interested in knowing how the area has changed over the years. If so, please read on.

Jenny and Jimmy Jarvis are now in their late sixties but they still like to reminisce about the happy times that they spent on the Eastmoor Estate all those years ago. Although Jenny married and moved away from the area in 1960 she continued to visit her parents, who remained there until 1980. Jimmy also married and moved away, but he too continued to visit his parents. He qualified as a teacher in 1961 and when the new Eastmoor High School opened its doors in 1968 he took up a post there. Here he had the unusual role of teaching children whose parents he himself had gone to school with, and played with as a child on the estate. Parents' Evenings often started with, 'Hi yer, Jimmy. How are yer? How's our Johnny behaving himself? If he isn't you've got my permission to give him a clip round the ear...Don't forget.' It was an excellent way to start the interview. It also made it easier for Jimmy to tell the parent that their Johnny was in fact a right little troublemaker. Jimmy retired from teaching in 1989 after twenty one enjoyable years at the school.

The biggest change to the Eastmoor area took place in the late 1940s and early 1950s when the estate was almost doubled in size, most of the building taking place on land to the east of the existing estate, either side of Windhill Road, and also between it and the single track railway line that carried coal from Parkhills Pit to the Pit Yard.

A whole series of changes then took place over the years, so that today Eastmoor is a very different place. These changes were inevitable, but the Eastmoor people may be divided as to whether they have been for the benefit of the area or not. Not now living there, Jenny and Jimmy felt that it would be unfair to express an opinion. Jimmy does, however, still have friends who teach at the

High School, and all indications are that the Eastmoor area is a thriving community, with a lot going for it.

So, what are the changes that have taken place? Well, the brickworks was closed many years ago and the quarry filled in. The area is now grassed over and is a children's playground. There is also a floodlit all-weather area for playing ball games. The Old Quarry was also filled in and grassed over, but even with a good fall of snow it is hard to imagine that it would make a good 'sledge run' as it undoubtedly was when Jenny and Jimmy were children. Park Lodge Lane is a main road. If it too were covered with snow, the gritting wagons would be there long before the first sledge. The two pits have gone, with little sign that they ever existed at all. This was inevitable as coal reserves became used up or difficult to mine. Much sadness was expressed locally when the mines closed. The pit heap was removed, and Little Wood, such a magical, natural play area for children, disappeared at the same time.

The Pit Yard, Gelder's Field and Devil's Hollow are now covered with houses, but funnily enough, the Long Wall still remains. Much is covered with climbing shrubs and in most parts difficult to see. The large King George playing field accommodates the Eastmoor Dragons Amateur Rugby League Club. There is now a large clubhouse and a floodlit pitch. There is also a fenced off football pitch.

The two hospitals - Stanley Royd and the County, that served the area so well over many years, are now closed and have been, or are in the process of being converted into private housing. But the horse chestnut trees in the Stanley Royd grounds are still producing their conkers and growing even taller.

The river and canal have changed very little over the years, but the area of land between them certainly has. The sand quarry (Tony Steel never quite made it across the Channel, but he did swim across Morcambe Bay, a distance of about eleven miles) was filled in many years ago, and the whole area is now the largest landfill site in the whole of the country, some say even in Europe. One can only guess at the price the residents of Eastmoor will ultimately have to pay for what appeared to be a foolhardy decision by the local Council to allow this to go ahead. One thing is certain, most, if not all, of the residents are of the opinion that this is one development that has been to the detriment of the whole area. The weir is still there, and there is even talk of a power station being built on it to produce electricity from the fast flowing water.

The Carlton and Empire cinemas were closed and demolished many years ago, but Kirkgate Station is still open. The horses were replaced by a shunter when they retired. Hopefully they spent their final years running around some large grassy field. The line through the station in now, however, only a minor one, and no self respecting rail enthusiast (they aren't called trainspotters any more) would be seen dead there. Long gone are the days when The Boat Train passed through carrying its passengers from Newcastle and York to Liverpool. The Ninety Nine Arches are as important as they were all those years ago. The line has now been electrified and carries the high speed trains from Leeds to London.

In the 1950s a large Primary School, Heath View, was built in the centre of the estate. A Secondary School, Eastmoor High, built close by, was opened in 1968. It is now called Wakefield City High.

One of the most worthwhile developments that have taken place is the Eastmoor Community Project. It was founded in 1995-6 and was originally based at Heath View School. As the community development role of the project expanded new premises were required. In 1999 a decision was taken by the Church of St Andrew's and St Swithin's to donate the old St Swithin's land and property back to the community and in September 2003 the St Swithin's Community Centre was opened. Its Aims are to generate and maintain community involvement, with emphasis on education, training and health issues.

So, there you have it. You now know as much as I do about the lives of Jenny and Jimmy Jarvis, the home in which they spent the first twenty or so years of their lives, a little about their parents, and something about the Eastmoor area where they lived. You also know how the area has changed over the years, and how it is today. There is little doubt that the lifestyles of Jenny and Jimmy were very different from those of children today, But were they as happy as today's children? Well, it is their undoubted opinion that they were, maybe even more so, simply because there are pressures on today's young people that were not on them. There were no continuous battles about ear piercing, sleep overs and designer labels. In fact Jenny's mother made a lot of clothes for her daughter. How many mothers would, or could do so today? And if they could, just imagine their daughter's response.

'If you think I'm going to wear that, you're very much mistaken.'

Jimmy's arguments with his dad weren't about whether or not he could have the latest strip of his favourite football team, complete with a name and number on the back, or a pair of designer trainers, but whether or not he could paint his bike bright yellow, or use the garden shed as his gang's headquarters. An interesting question would be - would today's children like to have lived in the same street as Jenny and Jimmy way back in 1947? I suspect that they would not. Neither would Jenny and Jimmy have like to have lived with children way back in 1897. I'm sure that all our country's children think that the times in which they live are the best. And that's how it should be. There may be some parts of the world, however, where the children, knowing the conditions that prevailed in their country fifty years ago, would willingly go back to that time, for example in areas crippled by famine or war, and I hope that you would agree with me that if that were to be the case then it would be a very sad state of affairs.

I hope that you enjoyed your brief look at how Jenny and Jimmy Jarvis lived their lives way back in the late 1940s. Was it an exciting time for them? They say without doubt that it was. Would you have found it exciting living at that time on the Eastmoor Estate? Well...only you can answer that question.

Your friend the author - David T Craggs